The Surfing Goat

Goatee

Featuring
Pismo the Kid

WHAT DOES THE GOAT SAY "?

MEEEHH!

by Dana Joseph McGregor
Illustrated by Ish Abdullah

Love

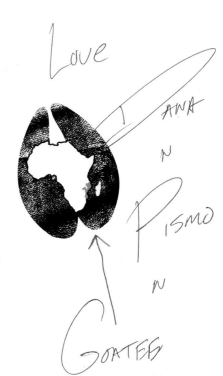

DANA N PISMO N GOATEE

Scripture taken from the Holy Bible, NEW INTERNATIONAL VERSION®. Copyright © 1973, 1978, 1984 by Biblica, Inc. All rights reserved worldwide. Used by permission. NEW INTERNATIONAL VERSION® and NIV® are registered trademarks of Biblica, Inc. Use of either trademark for the offering of goods or services requires the prior written consent of Biblica US, Inc.

A special thanks to our amazing photographers:
Jonah & Lindsay jonahandlindsay.com
Vincent Shay vincentshayphotography.com
Ben & Maureen Schutzer RunAmuckphotography.com
Giuseppe DeMasi demasiphotography.com
Ish Abdullah ishcreatives.com

WestBow Press books may be ordered through booksellers or by contacting:
WestBow Press
A Division of Thomas Nelson & Zondervan
1663 Liberty Drive
Bloomington, IN 47403
www.westbowpress.com
1 (866) 928-1240

ISBN: 978-1-5127-1350-3 (sc)
ISBN: 978-1-5127-1349-7 (e)
Library of Congress Control Number: 2015915588

Print information available on the last page.

WestBow Press rev. date: 10/29/2015

Dedicated to my niece McKenna McGregor and my cousin Josh Ainsworth.

WestBow
PRESS®
A DIVISION OF THOMAS NELSON
& ZONDERVAN

Once upon a time,

in a land called Pismo Beach.

There lived a man, who had a plan

to help his mom clear her yard of poison oak and weeds.

He would itch and scratch for months on end;

he thought that he would never win.

So he said to himself,

"I have an idea, I can get a goat to eat the weeds and never itch again!"

The man got in his car and off he drove to find himself a goat.
But there were so many to choose from, he kind of lost hope.

He said to the goat farmer, "I want one to eat all my weeds,
and then I would like to eat the goat, with my friends from Mozambique."
So he prayed to God and asked Him,
"Which one should I get?" All of a sudden, there she was; she walked right up to him!
She was beautiful and friendly and as gentle as a goat could be.
She had long white hair on her chinny chin chin, so he named her Goatee.

He put her in the back of the car and headed toward home.
She amazed a lot of people that were driving on the road.
The people laughed, smiled and screamed;
they couldn't believe what they had seen.
"There's a goat in your car" or "nice dog" they would say
but the funniest of all was, "I've seen it all today!"

They arrived at home, worked day and night
and Goatee and the man got really tight.
But the plan did not work too well. He kept getting poison oak
because every time he tucked her in at night, he would rub her beautiful coat.
He couldn't sleep. He tossed and turned.
He scratched his skin until it burned.

What he thought would take a month took an entire year,
and they grew so close that the idea of "barbecued Goatee" brought a tear!

...to the soccer field,

...to church,

...and even to the sea.

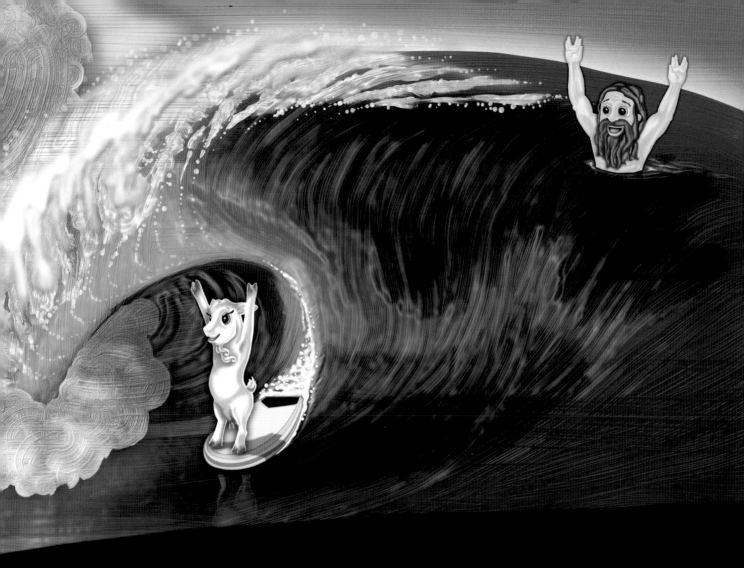

Then one day he had a thought, "I wonder if she could surf?"

So he paddled her out into a wave, and everyone said "Noooooo waaaayyy!!!!"

The local news showed up to see this prodigy.

Hanging four hooves all the way in, was "The Surfing Goat, Goatee."

She made the news from London to L.A.

and everywhere in between. She became famous in a day!

Although Goatee was neither great nor fast at eating up the weeds,
and the man kept getting poison oak, like a very baaaaaad dream,
and even though he and his friends did not get to barbecue Goatee,
the man heard God speak to his heart saying "Goatee is a gift from Me."

They raised money for a goat farm for the poor in Mozambique
and Goatee went on to become a celebrity of Pismo Beach.
She had a son and named him Pismo, who loved to surf more than she,
who soon became the greatest Surfing Goat there ever was to be.

So this is just the beginning for the Surfing Goat family.
There will be many more adventures to come, but until then remember this one thing...
When the weeds of life surround you and your plan does not work out the way you like,
God might just have a surprise for you, that will change your life!